The Key Facts™ on

Nigeria

Essential Information on Nigeria

By Patrick W. Nee

The Internationalist®

www.internationalist.com

The Internationalist®

International Business, Investment, and Travel

Published by:

The Internationalist Publishing Company

96 Walter Street/ Suite 200

Boston, MA 02131, USA

Tel: 617-354-7722

www.internationalist.com

PN@internationalist.com

Table Of Contents

Chapter 1: Background

British influence and control over what would become Nigeria and Africa's most populous country grew through the 19th century. A series of constitutions after World War II granted Nigeria greater autonomy; independence came in 1960. Following nearly 16 years of military rule, a new constitution was adopted in 1999, and a peaceful transition to civilian government was completed. The government continues to face the daunting task of reforming a petroleum-based economy, whose revenues have been squandered through corruption and mismanagement, and institutionalizing democracy. In addition, Nigeria continues to experience longstanding ethnic and religious tensions. Although both the 2003 and 2007 presidential elections were marred by significant irregularities and violence, Nigeria is currently experiencing its longest period of civilian rule since independence. The general elections of April 2007 marked the first civilian-to-civilian transfer of power in the country's history and the elections of 2011 were generally regarded as credible. In January 2014, Nigeria assumed a nonpermanent seat on the UN Security Council for the 2014-15 term.

Chapter 2: Geography

Location:

Western Africa, bordering the Gulf of Guinea, between Benin and Cameroon

Geographic coordinates:

10 00 N, 8 00 E

Map references:

Africa

Area:

total: 923,768 sq km

country comparison to the world: 32

land: 910,768 sq km

water: 13,000 sq km

Area - comparative:

slightly more than twice the size of California

Land boundaries:

total: 4,047 km

border countries: Benin 773 km, Cameroon 1,690 km, Chad 87 km, Niger 1,497 km

Coastline:

853 km

Maritime claims:

territorial sea: 12 nm

exclusive economic zone: 200

continental shelf: 200 m depth or to the deph of exploitation

Climate:

varies; equatorial in south, tropical in center, arid in north

Terrain:

southern lowlands merge into central hills and plateaus; mountains in southeast, plains in north

Elevation extremes:

lowest point: Atlantic Ocean 0 m

highest point: Chappal Waddi 2,419 m

Natural resources:

natural gas, petroleum, tin, iron ore, coal, limestone, niobium, lead, zinc, arable land

Land use:

arable land: 38.97%

permanent crops: 3.46%

other: 57.57% (2011)

Irrigated land:

2,932 sq km (2004)

Total renewable water resources:

286.2 cu km (2011)

Freshwater withdrawal (domestic/industrial/agricultural):

total: 13.11 cu km/yr (31%/15%/54%)

per capita: 89.21 cu m/yr (2005)

Natural hazards:

periodic droughts; flooding

Environment - current issues:

soil degradation; rapid deforestation; urban air and water pollution; desertification; oil pollution - water, air, and soil; has suffered serious damage from oil spills; loss of arable land; rapid urbanization

Environment - international agreements:

party to: Biodiversity, Climate Change, Climate Change-Kyoto Protocol, Desertification, Endangered Species, Hazardous Wastes, Law of the Sea, Marine Dumping, Marine Life Conservation, Ozone Layer Protection, Ship Pollution, Wetlands

signed, but not ratified: none of the selected agreements

Geography - note:

the Niger enters the country in the northwest and flows southward through tropical rain forests and swamps to its delta in the Gulf of Guinea

Chapter 3: People and Society

Nationality:

noun: Nigerian(s)

adjective: Nigerian

Ethnic groups:

Nigeria, Africa's most populous country, is composed of more than 250 ethnic groups; the following are the most populous and politically influential: Hausa and Fulani 29%, Yoruba 21%, Igbo (Ibo) 18%, Ijaw 10%, Kanuri 4%, Ibibio 3.5%, Tiv 2.5%

Languages:

English (official), Hausa, Yoruba, Igbo (Ibo), Fulani, over 500 additional indigenous languages

Religions:

Muslim 50%, Christian 40%, indigenous beliefs 10%

Population:

177,155,754 (July 2014 est.)

country comparison to the world: 8

note: estimates for this country explicitly take into account the effects of excess mortality due to AIDS; this can result in lower life expectancy, higher infant mortality, higher death rates, lower population growth rates, and changes in the distribution of population by age and sex than would otherwise be expected

Age structure:

0-14 years: 43.2% (male 39,151,304/female 37,353,737)

15-24 years: 19.3% (male 17,486,117/female 16,732,533)

25-54 years: 30.5% (male 27,697,644/female 26,285,816)

55-64 years: 3.1% (male 3,393,631/female 3,571,301)

65 years and over: 3% (male 2,621,845/female 2,861,826)

(2014 est.)

Dependency ratios:

total dependency ratio: 89 %

youth dependency ratio: 83.8 %

elderly dependency ratio: 5.2 %

potential support ratio: 19.3 (2013)

Median age:

total: 18.2 years

male: 18.1 years

female: 18.3 years (2014 est.)

Population growth rate:

2.47% (2014 est.)

country comparison to the world: 33

Birth rate:

38.03 births/1,000 population (2014 est.)

country comparison to the world: 12

Death rate:

13.16 deaths/1,000 population (2014 est.)

country comparison to the world: 19

Net migration rate:

-0.22 migrant(s)/1,000 population (2014 est.)

country comparison to the world: 120

Urbanization:

urban population: 49.6% of total population (2011)

rate of urbanization: 3.75% annual rate of change (2010-15 est.)

Major urban areas - population:

Lagos 10.203 million; Kano 3.304 million; Ibadan 2.762 million; ABUJA (capital) 1.857 million; Kaduna 1.519 million (2009)

Sex ratio:

at birth: 1.06 male(s)/female

0-14 years: 1.05 male(s)/female

15-24 years: 1.05 male(s)/female

25-54 years: 1.05 male(s)/female

55-64 years: 1.04 male(s)/female

65 years and over: 0.85 male(s)/female

total population: 1.01 male(s)/female (2014 est.)

Mother's mean age at first birth:

20.9 (2008 est.)

Maternal mortality rate:

630 deaths/100,000 live births (2010)

country comparison to the world: 11

Infant mortality rate:

    <u>total</u>: 74.09 deaths/1,000 live births

    <u>country comparison to the world</u>: 10

    <u>male</u>: 79.02 deaths/1,000 live births

    <u>female</u>: 68.87 deaths/1,000 live births (2014 est.)

Life expectancy at birth:

    <u>total population</u>: 52.62 years

    <u>country comparison to the world</u>: 212

    <u>male</u>: 51.63 years

    <u>female</u>: 53.66 years (2014 est.)

Total fertility rate:

    5.25 children born/woman (2014 est.)

    <u>country comparison to the world</u>: 13

Contraceptive prevalence rate:

    14.1% (2011)

Health expenditures:

    5.3% of GDP (2011)

    <u>country comparison to the world</u>: 127

Physicians density:

    0.4 physicians/1,000 population (2008)

Hospital bed density:

    0.53 beds/1,000 population (2004)

Drinking water source:

improved:

urban: 75.1% of population

rural: 47.3% of population

total: 61.1% of population

unimproved:

urban: 24.9% of population

rural: 52.7% of population

total: 38.9% of population (2011 est.)

Sanitation facility access:

improved:

urban: 33.2% of population

rural: 28.1% of population

total: 30.6% of population

unimproved:

urban: 66.8% of population

rural: 71.9% of population

total: 69.4% of population (2011 est.)

HIV/AIDS - adult prevalence rate:

3.1% (2012 est.)

country comparison to the world: 20

HIV/AIDS - people living with HIV/AIDS:

3,426,600 (2012 est.)

country comparison to the world: 2

HIV/AIDS - deaths:

239,700 (2012 est.)

country comparison to the world: 1

Major infectious diseases:

degree of risk: very high

food or waterborne diseases: bacterial and protozoal diarrhea, hepatitis A and E, and typhoid fever

vectorborne diseases: malaria, dengue fever, and yellow fever

water contact diseases: leptospirosis and schistosomiasis

respiratory disease: meningococcal meningitis

aerosolized disit or soil contact disease: one of the most highly endemic areas for Lassa fever

animal contact disease: ravies

ntoe: highly pathogenic H5N1 avian influenza has been identified in this country; it poses a negligible risk with extremely rare cases possible among US citizens who have close contact with birds (2013)

Obesity - adult prevalence rate:

6.5% (2008)

country comparison to the world: 146

Children under the age of 5 underweight:

24.4% (2011)

country comparison to the world: 26

Education expenditures:

NA

Literacy:

definition: age 15 and over can read and write

total population: 61.3%

male: 72.1%

female: 50.4% (2010 est.)

School life expectancy (primary to tertiary education):

total: 9 years

male: 10 years

female: 8 years (2005)

Child labor – children ages 5-14:

total number: 11,396,823

percentage: 29% (2007 est.)

Chapter 4: Government and Key Leaders

Country name:

conventional long form: Federal Republic of Nigeria

conventional short form: Nigeria

Government type:

federal republic

Capital:

name: Abuja

geographic coordinates: 9 05 N, 7 32 E

time difference: UTC+1 (6 hours ahead of Washington, DC during Standard Time)

Administrative divisions:

36 states and 1 territory*; Abia, Adamawa, Akwa Ibom, Anambra, Bauchi, Bayelsa, Benue, Borno, Cross River, Delta, Ebonyi, Edo, Ekiti, Enugu, Federal Capital Territory*, Gombe, Imo, Jigawa, Kaduna, Kano, Katsina, Kebbi, Kogi, Kwara, Lagos, Nasarawa, Niger, Ogun, Ondo, Osun, Oyo, Plateau, Rivers, Sokoto, Taraba, Yobe, Zamfara

Independence:

1 October 1960 (from the UK)

National holiday:

Independence Day (National Day), 1 October (1960)

Constitution:

> several previous; latest adopted 5 May 1999, effective 29 May 1999; amended 2010 (2010)

Legal system:

> mixed legal system of English common law, Islamic law (in 12 northern states), and traditional law

International law organization participation:

> accepts compulsory ICJ jurisdiction with reservations; accepts ICCt jurisdiction

Suffrage:

> 18 years of age; universal

Executive branch:

> chief of state: President Goodluck JONATHAN (since 5 May 2010, acting since 9 February 2010); Vice President Mohammed Namadi SAMBO (since 19 May 2010); note - the president is both the chief of state and head of government; JONATHAN assumed the presidency on 5 May 2010 following the death of President YAR'ADUA; JONATHAN was elected president on 16 April 2011
>
> head of government: President Goodluck JONATHAN (since 5 May 2010, acting since 9 February 2010); Vice President Mohammed Namadi SAMBO (since 19 May 2010)
>
> cabinet: Federal Executive Council

elections: president elected by popular vote for a four-year term (eligible for a second term); election last held on 16 April 2011 (next to be held in February 2015)

election results: Goodluck JONATHAN elected president; percent of vote - Goodluck JONATHAN 58.9%, Muhammadu BUHARI 32.0%, Nuhu RIBADU 5.4%, Ibrahim SHEKARAU 2.4%, other 1.3%

Legislative branch:

bicameral National Assembly consists of the Senate (109 seats, 3 from each state plus 1 from Abuja; members elected by popular vote to serve four-year terms) and House of Representatives (360 seats; members elected by popular vote to serve four-year terms)

elections: Senate - last held on 9 and 26 April 2011 (next to be held in February 2015); House of Representatives - last held on 9 and 26 April 2011 (next to be held in February 2015)

election results: Senate - percent of vote by party - NA; seats by party - PDP 73, ACN 17, ANPP 7, CPC 6, LP 4, other 2; House of Representatives - percent of vote by party - NA; seats by party - PDP 205, ACN 69, CPC 36, ANPP 28, LP 9, APGA 6, ACC 5, other 2; note - due to logistical problems elections in a number of constituencies were held on 26 April 2011

Judicial branch:

Highest court(s): Supreme Court (consists of the chief justice and 15 justices)

Judge selection and term of offfice: judges appointed by the president on the recommendation of the National Judicial Council, a 23-member independent body of federal and state judicial officials; judge appointments confirmed by the Senate; judges serve until age 65

subordinate courts: Court of Appeal; Federal High Court; High Court of the Federal Capital Territory; Sharia Court of Appeal of the Federal Capital Territory; Customary Court of Appeal of the Federal Capital Territory; state court system similar in structure to federal system

Political parties and leaders:

Accord Party or ACC [Mohammad Lawal MALADO]

Action Congress of Nigeria or ACN [Adebisi Bamidele AKANDE]

All Nigeria Peoples Party or ANPP [Ogbonnaya C. ONU]

All Progressives Congress [Adebisi Bamidele AKANDE, acting]

All Progressives Grand Alliance or APGA [Victor C. UMEH]

Congress for Progressive Change or CPC [Tony MOMOH]

Democratic Peoples Party or DPP [Jeremiah USENI]

Labor Party [Chief Dan NWANYANWU]

Peoples Democratic Party or PDP [Adamu MU'AZU]

Political pressure groups and leaders:

Academic Staff Union for Universities or ASUU

Campaign for Democracy or CD

Civil Liberties Organization or CLO

Committee for the Defense of Human Rights or CDHR

Constitutional Right Project or CRP

Human Right Africa

National Association of Democratic Lawyers or NADL

National Association of Nigerian Students or NANS

Nigerian Bar Association or NBA

Nigerian Labor Congress or NLC

Nigerian Medical Association or NMA

the press

Universal Defenders of Democracy or UDD

International organization participation:

ACP, AfDB, AU, C, CD, D-8, ECOWAS, EITI (compliant country), FAO, G-15, G-24, G-77, IAEA, IBRD, ICAO, ICC (national committees), ICRM, IDA, IDB, IFAD, IFC, IFRCS, IHO, ILO, IMF, IMO, IMSO, Interpol, IOC, IOM, IPU, ISO, ITSO, ITU, ITUC (NGOs), MIGA, MINURSO,

MINUSMA, MONUSCO, NAM, OAS (observer), OIC, OPCW, OPEC, PCA, UN, UN Security Council (temporary), UNAMID, UNCTAD, UNESCO, UNHCR, UNIDO, UNIFIL, UNISFA, UNITAR, UNMIL, UNMISS, UNOCI, UNWTO, UPU, WCO, WFTU (NGOs), WHO, WIPO, WMO, WTO

Diplomatic representation in the US:

chief of mission: Ambassador Adebowale Ibidapo ADEFUYE (since 26 March 2010)

chancery: 3519 International Court NW, Washington, DC 20008

telephone: [1] (202) 986-8400

FAX: [1] (202) 362-6541

consulate(s) general: Atlanta, New York

Diplomatic representation from the US:

chief of mission: Ambassador James F. ENTWISTLE (since 28 October 2013)

embassy: Plot 1075 Diplomatic Drive, Central District Area, Abuja

mailing address: P. O. Box 5760, Garki, Abuja

telephone: [234] (9) 461-4000

FAX: [234] (9) 461-4171

Key Leaders:

Pres.	Goodluck JONATHAN
Vice Pres.	Namadi SAMBO
Min. of Agriculture & Natural Resources	Akinwunmi Ayo ADESINA, *Dr.*
Min. of Aviation	Stella ODUAH-OGIEMWONYI
Min. of Communication Technology	Omobola Johnson OLUBUSOLA
Min. of Culture & Tourism	Edem DUKE
Min. of Defense	Bello MOHAMMED
Min. of Education	Raqayyatu Ahmed RUFAI
Min. of Environment	Hadiza Ibrahim MAILAFA
Min. of the Federal Capital Territory	Bala MOHAMMED
Min. of Finance	Ngozi OKONJO-IWEALA
Min. of Foreign Affairs	Olugbenga Ayodeji ASHIRU
Min. of Health	Onyebuchi CHUKWU
Min. of Industry, Trade, & Investment	Olusegun AGANGA
Min. of Information & Communications	Labaran MAKU
Min. of Interior	Abba MORO
Min. of Justice & Attorney Gen. of the Federation	Mohammed Bello ADOKE
Min. of Labor & Productivity	Chukwuemeka Ngozichineke WOGU
Min. of Lands, Housing, & Development	Ama PEPPLE
Min. of Mines & Steel Development	Musa Mohammed SADA
Min. of National Planning Commission	Shamsudeen USMAN
Min. of National Sports Commission	Ibrahim Isa BIO
Min. for the Niger Delta Affairs	Peter Godsday ORUBEBE

Min. of Petroleum Resources	Diezani ALISON-MADUEKE
Min. of Police Affairs	Caleb OLUBOLADE, *Capt. (Ret.)*
Min. of Power	Chinedu Ositadinma NEBO
Min. of Science & Technology	Ita Okon Bassey EWA
Min. of Special Duties	Ernest OLUBOLADE
Min. of Sports	Yusuf SULEIMAN
Min. of Transport	Idris UMAR
Min. of Water Resources	Sarah Reng OCHEKPE
Min. of Women's Affairs	Josephine ANENIH
Min. of Works	Mike ONOLEMEMEN
Min. of Youth Development	Bolaji ABDULLAHI
Governor, Central Bank of Nigeria	Sanusi Lamido SANUSI
Ambassador to the US	Adebowale ADEFUYE
Permanent Representative to the UN, New York	Joy OGWU

Flag description:

three equal vertical bands of green (hoist side), white, and green; the color green represents the forests and abundant natural wealth of the country, white stands for peace and unity

National symbol(s):

eagle

National anthem:

name: "Arise Oh Compatriots, Nigeria's Call Obey"

lyrics/music: John A. ILECHUKWU, Eme Etim AKPAN, B. A. OGUNNAIKE, Sotu OMOIGUI and P. O. ADERIBIGBE/Benedict Elide ODIASE

<u>note</u>: adopted 1978; the lyrics are a mixture of five of the top entries in a national contest

Chapter 5: Economy

Economy - overview:

Following an April 2014 statistical "rebasing" exercise, Nigeria has emerged as Africa's largest economy, with 2013 GDP estimated at US$ 502 billion. Oil has been a dominant source of government revenues since the 1970s. Regulatory constraints and security risks have limited new investment in oil and natural gas, and Nigeria's oil production contracted in 2012 and 2013. Nevertheless, the Nigerian economy has continued to grow at a rapid 6-8% per annum (pre-rebasing), driven by growth in agriculture, telecommunications, and services, and the medium-term outlook for Nigeria is good, assuming oil output stabilizes and oil prices remain strong. Fiscal authorities pursued countercyclical policies in 2011-2013, significantly reducing the budget deficit. Monetary policy has also been responsive and effective. Following the 2008-9 global financial crises, the banking sector was effectively recapitalized and regulation enhanced. Despite its strong fundamentals, oil-rich Nigeria has been hobbled by inadequate power supply, lack of infrastructure, delays in the passage of legislative reforms, an inefficient property registration system, restrictive trade policies, an inconsistent regulatory environment, a slow and ineffective judicial system, unreliable dispute resolution mechanisms, insecurity, and pervasive corruption. Economic diversification and strong growth have not translated into a significant decline in poverty levels - over 62% of Nigeria's 170 million people live in extreme poverty. President JONATHAN has established an economic team that includes experienced and reputable members and has announced plans to increase transparency, continue to diversify production, and further improve fiscal management. The government is working to develop stronger public-private partnerships for roads, agriculture, and power.

GDP (purchasing power parity):

$478.5 billion (2013 est.)

country comparison to the world: 31

$450.4 billion (2012 est.)

$422.6 billion (2011 est.)

note: data are in 2013 US dollars

GDP (official exchange rate):

$292 billion (2013 est.)

GDP - real growth rate:

6.2% (2013 est.)

country comparison to the world: 35

6.6% (2012 est.)

7.4% (2011 est.)

GDP - per capita (PPP):

$2,800 (2013 est.)

country comparison to the world: 180

$2,700 (2012 est.)

$2,600 (2011 est.)

note: data are in 2013 US dollars

Gross national saving:

15.5% of GDP (2013 est.)

country comparison to the world: 108

15.9% of GDP (2012 est.)

15.4% of GDP (2011 est.)

GDP – composition, by end use:

household consumption: 50.3%

government consumption: 12.8%

investment in fixed capital: 9.8%

investment in inventories: 0%

exports of goods and services: 49.9%

imports of goods and services: -22.8% (2013 est.)

GDP - composition by sector:

agriculture: 30.9%

industry: 43%

services: 26% (2012 est.)

Agriculture – products:

cocoa, peanuts, cotton, palm oil, corn, rice, sorghum, millet, cassava (tapioca), yams, rubber; cattle, sheep, goats, pigs; timber; fish

Industries:

crude oil, coal, tin, columbite; rubber products, wood; hides and skins, textiles, cement and other construction materials, food products, footwear, chemicals, fertilizer, printing, ceramics, steel

Industrial production growth rate:

0.9% (2013 est.)

country comparison to the world: 155

Labor force:

51.53 million (2011 est.)

country comparison to the world: 12

Labor force - by occupation:

agriculture: 70%

industry: 10%

services: 20% (1999 est.)

Unemployment rate:

23.9% (2011 est.)

country comparison to the world: 172

4.9% (2011 est.)

Population below poverty line:

70% (2010 est.)

Household income or consumption by percentage share:

lowest 10%: 1.8%

highest 10%: 38.2% (2010 est.)

Distribution of family income - Gini index:

43.7 (2003)

country comparison to the world: 47

50.6 (1997)

Budget:

revenues: $23.85 billion

expenditures: $31.51 billion (2013 est.)

Taxes and other revenues:

8.2% of GDP (2013 est.)

country comparison to the world: 211

Budget surplus (+) or deficit (-):

-2.6% of GDP (2013 est.)

country comparison to the world: 109

Public debt:

19.3% of GDP (2013 est.)

country comparison to the world: 135

17.9% of GDP (2012 est.)

Inflation rate (consumer prices):

8.7% (2013 est.)

country comparison to the world: 200

12.2% (2012 est.)

Central bank discount rate:

4.25% (31 December 2010 est.)

country comparison to the world: 59

6% (31 December 2009 est.)

Commercial bank prime lending rate:

15.5% (31 December 2013 est.)

country comparison to the world: 33

16.79% (31 December 2012 est.)

Stock of narrow money:

$46.48 billion (31 December 2013 est.)

country comparison to the world: 49

$44.41 billion (31 December 2012 est.)

Stock of broad money:

$98.75 billion (31 December 2013 est.)

country comparison to the world: 53

$96.34 billion (31 December 2012 est.)

Stock of domestic credit:

$93.46 billion (31 December 2013 est.)

country comparison to the world: 53

$93.5 billion (31 December 2012 est.)

Market value of publicly traded shares:

$56.39 billion (31 December 2012 est.)

country comparison to the world: 54

$39.27 billion (31 December 2011)

$50.88 billion (31 December 2010 est.)

Current account balance:

$16.16 billion (2013 est.)

country comparison to the world: 19

$20.35 billion (2012 est.)

Exports:

$93.55 billion (2013 est.)

<u>country comparison to the world</u>: 38

$95.68 billion (2012 est.)

Exports - commodities:

petroleum and petroleum products 95%, cocoa, rubber

Exports - partners:

US 16.8%, India 11.5%, Netherlands 8.6%, Spain 7.8%, Brazil 7.6%, UK 5.1%, Germany 4.9%, Japan 4.1%, France 4.1% (2012)

Imports:

$55.98 billion (2013 est.)

<u>country comparison to the world</u>: 52

$53.36 billion (2012 est.)

Imports - commodities:

machinery, chemicals, transport equipment, manufactured goods, food and live animals

Imports - partners:

China 18.3%, US 10.1%, India 5.5% (2012)

Reserves of foreign exchange and gold:

$47.7 billion (31 December 2013 est.)

<u>country comparison to the world</u>: 43

$46.41 billion (31 December 2012 est.)

Debt - external:

$15.73 billion (31 December 2013 est.)

country comparison to the world: 86

$13.4 billion (31 December 2012 est.)

Exchange rates:

Nairas (NGN) per US dollar -

156.8 (2013 est.)

156.81 (2012 est.)

150.3 (2010 est.)

148.9 (2009)

117.8 (2008)

Chapter 6: Energy

Electricity - production:

24.87 billion kWh (2010 est.)

country comparison to the world: 68

Electricity - consumption:

20.38 billion kWh (2010 est.)

country comparison to the world: 69

Electricity - exports:

0 kWh (2012 est.)

country comparison to the world: 177

Electricity - imports:

0 kWh (2012 est.)

country comparison to the world: 178

Electricity - installed generating capacity:

5.9 million kW (2010 est.)

country comparison to the world: 72

Electricity - from fossil fuels:

67.1% of total installed capacity (2010 est.)

country comparison to the world: 114

Electricity - from nuclear fuels:

0% of total installed capacity (2010 est.)

country comparison to the world: 151

Electricity - from hydroelectric plants:

32.8% of total installed capacity (2010 est.)

country comparison to the world: 70

Electricity - from other renewable sources:

0% of total installed capacity (2010 est.)

country comparison to the world: 209

Crude oil - production:

2.524 million bbl/day (2012 est.)

country comparison to the world: 12

Crude oil - exports:

2.341 million bbl/day (2010 est.)

country comparison to the world: 5

Crude oil - imports:

0 bbl/day (2010 est.)

country comparison to the world: 104

Crude oil - proved reserves:

37.2 billion bbl (1 January 2013 es)

country comparison to the world: 10

Refined petroleum products - production:

101,300 bbl/day (2010 est.)

country comparison to the world: 73

Refined petroleum products - consumption:

271,600 bbl/day (2011 est.)

country comparison to the world: 46

Refined petroleum products - exports:

18,750 bbl/day (2010 est.)

country comparison to the world: 73

Refined petroleum products - imports:

151,700 bbl/day (2010 est.)

country comparison to the world:38

Natural gas - production:

31.36 billion cu m (2011 est.)

country comparison to the world: 29

Natural gas - consumption:

5.03 billion cu m (2010 est.)

country comparison to the world: 62

Natural gas - exports:

25.96 billion cu m (2011 est.)

country comparison to the world: 16

Natural gas - imports:

0 cu m (2011 est.)

country comparison to the world: 106

Natural gas - proved reserves:

5.153 trillion cu m (1 January 2013 es)

country comparison to the world: 9

Carbon dioxide emissions from consumption of energy:

75.96 million Mt (2011 est.)

country comparison to the world: 47

Chapter 7: Communications

Telephones - main lines in use:

418,200 (2012)

country comparison to the world: 102

Telephones - mobile cellular:

112.78 million (2012)

country comparison to the world: 10

Telephone system:

general assessment: further expansion and modernization
of the fixed-line telephone network is needed; network
quality remains a problem

domestic: the addition of a second fixed-line provider in
2002 resulted in faster growth but subscribership remains
only about 1 per 100 persons; mobile-cellular services
growing rapidly, in part responding to the shortcomings of
the fixed-line network; multiple cellular providers operate
nationally with subscribership base approaching 60 per
100 persons

international: country code - 234; landing point for the
SAT-3/WASC fiber-optic submarine cable that provides
connectivity to Europe and Asia; satellite earth stations - 3
Intelsat (2 Atlantic Ocean and 1 Indian Ocean) (2010)

Broadcast media:

nearly 70 federal government-controlled national and regional TV stations; all 36 states operate TV stations; several private TV stations operational; cable and satellite TV subscription services are available; network of federal government-controlled national, regional, and state radio stations; roughly 40 state government-owned radio stations typically carry their own programs except for news broadcasts; about 20 private radio stations; transmissions of international broadcasters are available (2007)

Internet country code:

.ng

Internet hosts:

1,234 (2012)

country comparison to the world: 169

Internet users:

43.989 million (2009)

country comparison to the world: 9

Chapter 8: Transportation

Airports:

> 54 (2013)

> country comparison to the world: 87

Airports - with paved runways:

> total: 40

> over 3,047 m: 10

> 2,438 to 3,047 m: 12

> 1,524 to 2,437 m: 9

> 914 to 1,523 m: 6

> under 914 m: 3 (2013)

Airports - with unpaved runways:

> total: 14

> 1,524 to 2,437 m: 2

> 914 to 1,523 m: 9

> under 914 m: 3 (2013)

Heliports:

> 5 (2013)

Pipelines:

> condensate 124 km; gas 4,045 km; liquid petroleum gas 164 km; oil 4,441 km; refined products 3,940 km (2013)

Railways:

> total: 3,505 km

> country comparison to the world: 50

> narrow gauge: 3,505 km 1.067-m gauge (2008)

Roadways:

　　total: 7,705 km (2012)

　　country comparison to the world: 143

　　paved: 28,980 m

　　unpaved: 164,220 km (2004)

Waterways:

　　8,600 km (Niger and benue rivers and smaller rivers and creeks) (2011)

　　country comparison to the world: 15

Merchant marine:

　　total: 89

　　country comparison to the world: 54

　　by type: cargo 2, chemical tanker 28, liquefied gas 1, passenger/cargo 1, petroleum tanker 56, specialized tanker 1

　　foreign-owned: 3 (India 1, UK 2)

　　registered in other countries: 33 (Bahamas 2, Bermuda 11, Comoros 1, Italy 1, Liberia 4, North Korea 1, Panama 6, Seychelles 1, unknown 6) (2010)

Ports and terminals:

　　major seaport(s): Bonny Inshore Terminal, Calabar, Lagos

Transportation – note:

　　the International Maritime Bureau reports the territorial and offshore waters in the Niger Delta and Gulf of Guinea as high risk for piracy and armed robbery against ships; in 2012, 27 commercial vessels were boarded or attacked compared with 10 attacks in 2011; crews were robbed and stores or cargoes stolen; Nigerian pirates have extended the range of their attacks to as far away as Cote d'Ivoire

Chapter 9: Military

Military branches:

Nigerian Armed Forces: Army, Navy, Air Force (2013)

Military service age and obligation:

18 years of age for voluntary military service; no conscription (2012)

Manpower available for military service:

males age 16-49: 37,087,711

females age 16-49: 35,232,127 (2010 est.)

Manpower fit for military service:

males age 16-49: 20,839,976

females age 16-49: 19,867,683 (2010 est.)

Manpower reaching militarily significant age annually:

male: 1,767,428

female: 1,687,719 (2010 est.)

Military expenditures:

0.89% of GDP (2012)

country comparison to the world: 109

0.98% of GDP (2011)

0.89% of GDP (2010)

Chapter 10: Transnational Issues

Disputes - international:

> Joint Border Commission with Cameroon reviewed 2002 ICJ ruling on the entire boundary and bilaterally resolved differences, including June 2006 Greentree Agreement that immediately cedes sovereignty of the Bakassi Peninsula to Cameroon with a phase-out of Nigerian control within two years while resolving patriation issues; the ICJ ruled on an equidistance settlement of Cameroon-Equatorial Guinea-Nigeria maritime boundary in the Gulf of Guinea, but imprecisely defined coordinates in the ICJ decision and a sovereignty dispute between Equatorial Guinea and Cameroon over an island at the mouth of the Ntem River all contribute to the delay in implementation; only Nigeria and Cameroon have heeded the Lake Chad Commission's admonition to ratify the delimitation treaty which also includes the Chad-Niger and Niger-Nigeria boundaries; location of Benin-Niger-Nigeria tripoint is unresolved

Refugees and internally displaced persons:

> refugees (country of origin): 5,299 (Liberia) (2011)
>
> IDPs: undetermined (communal violence between Christians and Muslims, political violence; flooding; forced evictions; competition for resources; displacement is mostly short-term) (2012)

Illicit drugs:

a transit point for heroin and cocaine intended for European, East Asian, and North American markets; consumer of amphetamines; safe haven for Nigerian narcotraffickers operating worldwide; major money-laundering center; massive corruption and criminal activity; Nigeria has improved some anti-money-laundering controls, resulting in its removal from the Financial Action Task Force's (FATF's) Noncooperative Countries and Territories List in June 2006; Nigeria's anti-money-laundering regime continues to be monitored by FATF

Map of Nigeria

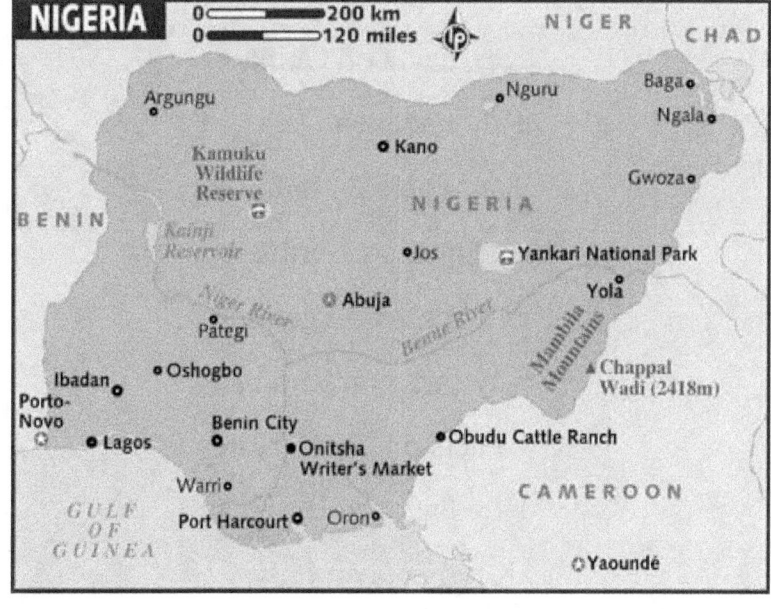

Other Key Facts™ Titles

Key Facts on South Korea

Key Facts on France

Key Facts on the United Kingdom

Key Facts on Egypt

Key Facts on Israel

All Key Facts™ Titles are Available at

www.Amazon.com

THE INTERNATIONALIST®

2014

WWW.INTERNATIONALIST.COM

www.ingramcontent.com/pod-product-compliance
Lightning Source LLC
Chambersburg PA
CBHW070714180526
45167CB00004B/1471